Series Editor: Rosalind Kerven

Heinemann Educational Publishers
Halley Court, Jordan Hill, Oxford OX2 8EJ

MADRID   ATHENS   PARIS
FLORENCE   PRAGUE   WARSAW
PORTSMOUTH NH   CHICAGO   SAO PAULO
SINGAPORE   TOKYO   MELBOURNE   AUCKLAND
IBADAN   GABORONE   JOHANNESBURG

© Heinemann Educational 1995

First published 1995

99 98 97 96 95
10 9 8 7 6 5 4 3 2 1

British Library Cataloguing in Publication Data
A catalogue record for this book is available from the British Library

Starter Pack
1 of each of 12 titles: ISBN 0 435 00957 5

Library Hardback
The Bharunda Bird: ISBN 0 431 06508 X
Pack 1 – 1 each of 6 titles: ISBN 0 431 06498 9
Pack 2 – 1 each of 6 titles: ISBN 0 431 06499 7

Typeset by Sue Vaudin
Printed and bound in Hong Kong

Acknowledgements
Title page and border illustration, pp 2/3: Hilary Evans; map, p2: Dave Bowyer; photographs, p3 (top): The British Library; (bottom): NHPA

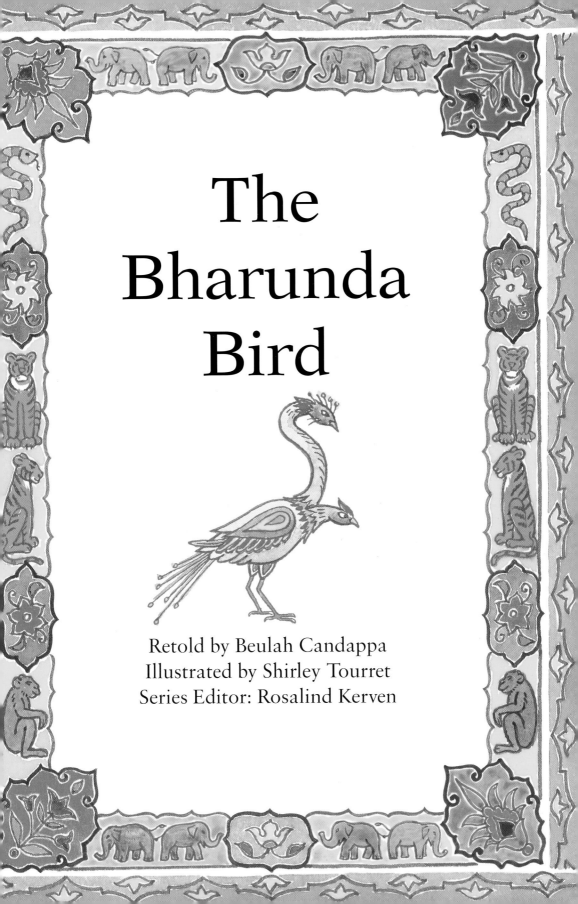

The Bharunda Bird

Retold by Beulah Candappa
Illustrated by Shirley Tourret
Series Editor: Rosalind Kerven

Introduction

The legend of The Bharunda Bird comes from India, one of the largest countries in the world. India has been one of the world's greatest civilizations for thousands of years.
It has many different peoples, languages and landscapes.
India is famous for its beautiful art, music, and delicious food.

Map of India

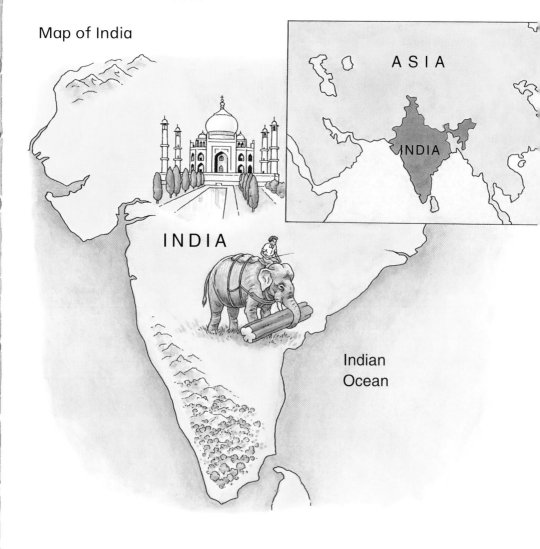

A Story with a Lesson

This story was first told
thousands of years ago.
It is from an
ancient book called
'The Panchatantra'.

This picture showing the
Bharunda bird was painted
about 500 years ago in India. ▶

The Bharunda Bird was told to
a king's lazy sons to teach
them worldly wisdom.
It is set in a tropical rain forest
in India like the forest here. ▼

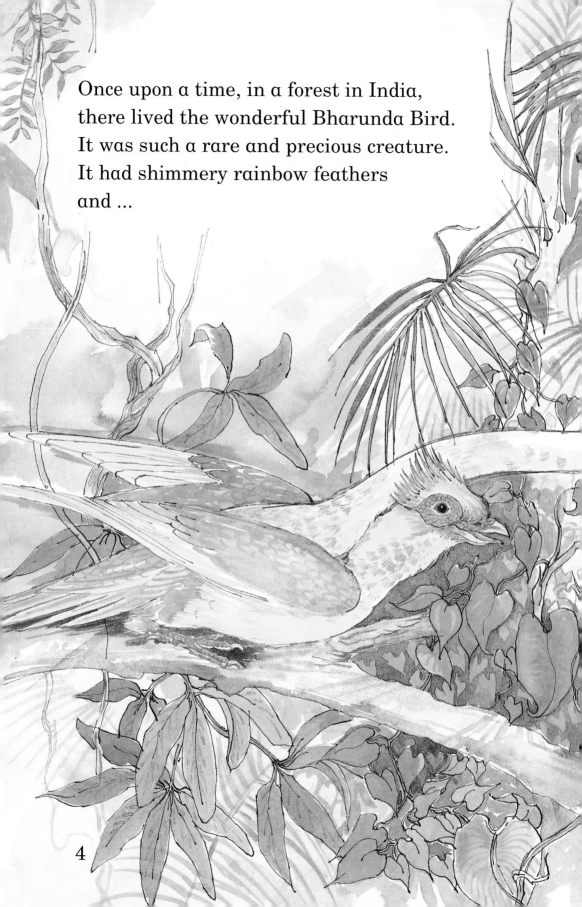

Once upon a time, in a forest in India,
there lived the wonderful Bharunda Bird.
It was such a rare and precious creature.
It had shimmery rainbow feathers
and ...

... two heads!
A tall head at the end of a long neck and
a short head at the end of a short neck.
The Bharunda Bird hid deep in the forest.
Very few people had ever seen it.
Those who had seen it would say:
"It must be our lucky day today!
We've seen the Bharunda Bird.
It's magic! Let's make a wish
for something special."

Now although the Bharunda Bird
looked different from all the
other birds in the forest,
it was a very happy bird.
The two heads were good friends
and they never stopped talking.
When one head asked a question:
"Ko-ko? Ko-ko-koo?"
the other head would answer:
"Kee-kee! Kee-Kee-Kee-KEE-EE!"

They shared everything.
When they were searching for food, the tall head
looked in front, while the short head looked behind.
The tall head would stretch his long neck out
and poke about the high branches.
And when he found delicious berries hiding there,
the tall head would call out to the short head:
"Best friend! You-way-down-there-near-the-earth!
Would you like to have some delicious berries?"

The short head would say:
"Snip-Snap!
Yes, please, best friend.
You know I'm always hungry!"
And the tall head would answer:
"Open your beak wide,
hungry fellow. Catch!"
And the short head would open
his beak wide:
"Snip-snap!" he would crunch up
the delicious berries.

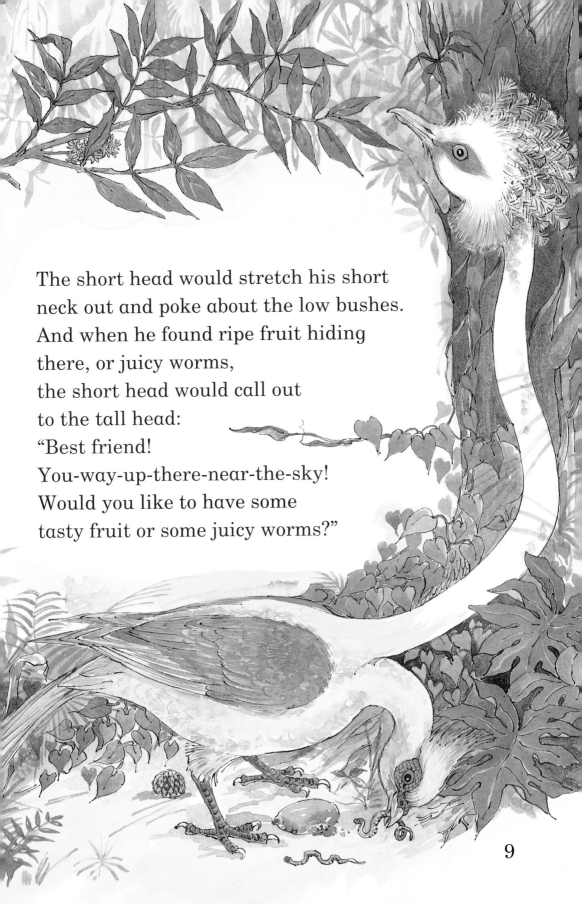

The short head would stretch his short
neck out and poke about the low bushes.
And when he found ripe fruit hiding
there, or juicy worms,
the short head would call out
to the tall head:
"Best friend!
You-way-up-there-near-the-sky!
Would you like to have some
tasty fruit or some juicy worms?"

9

And the tall head would say:
"Yum-yum! Yes, please, best
friend.
You know I love swallowing
juicy, slithery worms.
Just like spaghetti or noodles.
Yum-yum!"
And the short head
would say:
"Open your beak wide,
spaghetti-gobbler. Catch!"
And the tall head would open
his beak wide:
"Glib-glub!" he would gollop
up the juicy worms.

They sang together.
The tall head had a high voice:

"Ha-ha! Ha-ha-ha!"

And the short head had a low voice:

"Ho-ho! Ho-ho-ho!"

People said: "One sings high,
one sings low.
Together they sing in harmony.
'Ha-ha! Ho-ho!
Ha-ha-ha! Ho-ho-ho!'
They make such wonderful
music together.
Listen!"

Whenever they heard the Bharunda Bird singing,
the monkeys, the tigers, the elephants,
the bumble bees and the crocodiles stopped whatever
they were doing.
"Ahh!" they sighed. "It's the Bharunda Bird!
Listen to their harmonious singing!
Look how they share everything. It's wonderful!"

12

If two monkeys were arguing:
"Cha-cha! Cha-cha-cha-ah?" and pulling each other's tails, they would stop when they heard the beautiful singing.
Then they would put their arms around each other and go 'swingy-swinging' amongst the branches chattering happily:
"Cha-cha-cha-cha-cha-cha-cha!"
They would be friends once again.

Even if two tigers were growling: "Argh-aargh-aargh!"
and clawing each other,
when they heard the Bharunda Bird singing,
they would calm down, grow peaceful,
and go back into the forest side-by-side,
purring as softly as kittens:
"Urrr...urr...urrr!"

They would be friends once again.
Everybody in the forest was happy.

But, sad to say, one day the tall head
got angry with his best friend, the short head.
"You keep following me wherever I go," he shouted.
"Everyone likes to be alone sometimes,
but everywhere I go, you are there!
I wish you would leave me alone.
HA!"

Then he stopped sharing food with the short head,
and he stopped singing with him.

Soon the short head got angry too.

"You keep watching me whatever I do," he yelled.

"I'm fed up!

Can't I be private sometimes?

I wish you would mind your own business.

HO!"

After that the two heads began to hate each other.
They stopped sharing food.
They stopped singing together.
All they did was fight.
Everyone in the forest heard them and felt sad.
Soon the whole place was full
of fighting, squabbling creatures.

17

One day the tall head found some
delicious juice in a beautiful flower:
"Um-umm," he said. "This tastes like honey.
It's nectar... delicious. Um-umm!"
"Oh, give me some!" begged the short head.
"No!" screeched the tall head.
"I found it first. I'm not going to share.
It's all mine! Go away!"

"Don't be so selfish," snapped the short head.
"Don't I give you half of everything I find?
The ripe mangoes, the sweet custard apples,
the rosy pomegranates, the juicy worms?"
"All you give me is rotten fruit," squawked the
tall head, "and stupid, slow, slithery worms!
Anyone can find those by just looking on the ground.
But nectar. Umm-umm... that's different, that's rare.
Go and find your own!"

"Oh, please share, best friend, please,"
begged the short head.
"If you do, I promise I will give you
 something extra special soon,
something you have never dreamed of before."
"No!" screeched the tall head.
"I found it first. It's all mine. Go away!"
And he drank up more of the nectar.
The short head tried to get the nectar too
but he just couldn't reach.
He was so angry, he began to peck the tall head.
"Give me some! Greedy! Give me some!"
When the tall head felt the painful pecks,
he swooped down and pecked the short head back.
Both had sharp beaks.
Shimmery rainbow feathers were flying everywhere.

20

But the tall head was more cunning.
With his long neck he could swoop down,
peck his friend quickly and then swing his
long neck up again... and escape!
Oh dear! The short head, with his short
neck, was trapped.
Soon he was pecked so badly that his head
drooped limply down to the ground.
Doomph!
"Ha-ha!"
squawked the tall head.
"Serves you right!"
And he sucked up all the nectar!

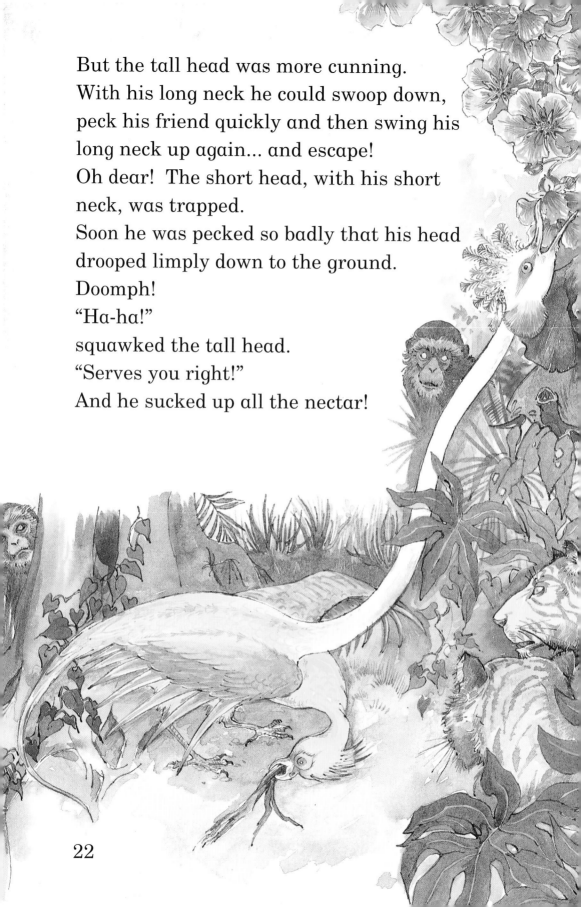

By now the short head was really angry.
His sharp eyes searched the forest floor
and found ...
a poisonous root growing on the ground.
He opened his beak, "Snip-snap!" and quickly
swallowed it.
Then he turned to the tall head.
"Ho-Ho!" he chuckled.
"Greedy one!
Now you'll be sorry.
I've just swallowed some poison.
Now **your** insides will burn like FIRE! Ho-Ho-Ho!"
What do you think happened next?

Yes!
The Bharunda Bird fell down... dead!
Silly heads!
They had forgotten that although they were two
separate heads, they shared the same stomach
so the poison killed them both.
What can we learn from the Bharunda Bird today?
Here's a little poem to start you thinking...

"The Bharunda Bird
Will teach us why
We should care for each other
Or wither and die.
One world, one life,
That's all we've got.
So, share...
Don't be greedy!
Don't grab the lot!"